Weighing the Present

Acknowledgements

Many thanks to the editors of the following magazines and websites: *Areté, Boneshaker, The Dark Horse, The North, The Poetry Review, The Rialto, The Spectator* and *Poetry International.* Special thanks too to The Poetry Trust for commissioning 'Treatment' as part of a residency in 2009 at the Norfolk and Norwich University Hospital and to the artist Ian Starsmore for commissioning 'Ladder' to accompany his 2013 exhibition at Cambridge University Library.

For Ian

in friendship
& with thanks
for the ladders
Michael
November 2014

Weighing the Present
Michael Laskey

smith|doorstop

Published 2014 by
smith|doorstop Books
The Poetry Business
Bank Street Arts
32-40 Bank Street
Sheffield S1 2DS
www.poetrybusiness.co.uk

ISBN 978-1-910367-03-2

British Library Cataloguing-in-Publication Data.
A catalogue record for this book is available from the
British Library.

Typeset by Utter
Printed by Printondemand.com
Cover image: Repairing the Bicycle by John Quinton Pringle
Author photo: Jovita Valaityte

smith|doorstop Books is a member of Inpress,
www.inpressbooks.co.uk. Distributed by Central Books Ltd.,
99 Wallis Road, London E9 5LN.

The Poetry Business is an Arts Council
National Portfolio Organisation

Supported by
ARTS COUNCIL
ENGLAND

Contents

Not That He Wrote Poems

but in the dream he'd been giving a reading,
launching his latest collection,
and once he was finished, with the audience
drifting off, he wondered out loud
if he'd sold any books. Oh dear friend.
Not only no queue, not a single
hanger-on to shield us from the view
of the stacked table. Precious few
dreams bring him back and yet
what did I go and do, but pretend
not to hear, then making myself wake up,
left him friendless, diminished there.

The Unexamined Life

I didn't look at the carcass
stretched on the road by my gate
any more than I had to know
the open-mouthed head and neck
twisted back was muntjac.

I wrapped myself up in the word,
a muffler against the cold,
and keeping close to the kerb
rode past on my bike,
intent on making the baker's

before they sold out of small browns,
loath even to imagine
bone spikes sliced through muscle
or the belly a staved in barrel
spilling out stuff.

And while I was gone, someone else –
from pity or driven to it
by the hold-up to the traffic or knowing
what venison's worth – got a grip
on its hooves, I suppose, and removed it.

Must Be About Now

she's due to go in for her hip
it occurs to him – he'll give her
a ring, although who knows,
she may already be home,
more or less able to hobble
along that hall to the phone.
An email would be better –
he might have an address,
he could check – but of course
what she'd like best, his old-
fashioned friend, is a letter.
How kind of him to have written,
to have taken the trouble, he imagines
her thinking as she unfolds it,
though he hasn't, and isn't, and won't.

Catch

Winter, dusk falling, long snow
frozen stiff in the tractor tracks
on the stubble field opposite,

yet it could still happen again,
you could drive through a city you're new to,
past parades of stubborn shops –

a butcher, hairdresser, chippy –
and beyond terraced houses the road
might open out, like then, by a rec

where cricket's going on: in their whites
most of them, and if the bus up ahead
would stop and allow you to watch

a ball or two, what a blessing,
but if not, it doesn't much matter –
the afternoon's looking up, *catch*.

Alternative

On the way to the office, in the dip
beyond Theberton, happening to glance
left through a gap in the hedge
up a track, an ungated gateway

in a moment I saw it all,
and so close to home, this unknown
fold in the land at right angles
to the road, a rising slope

of winter wheat, ploughed fields leading
to trees on a skyline I wanted
to climb to, to walk through and join
up with whatever's behind them.

Either ...

Or like him to say no more
milky coffee with two fingers
of KitKat to keep his weight up,
no more of that patient weekly
waiting for a vacant bed,
and no more reliably good
for nothing days afterwards.
Like him to choose instead
a last summer, almost
perfectly hopeless, but his.

A Breath

It was next to nothing, a ripple
of air, a breath of a breeze
through the window, open a little
at the top, that brushed across
my forehead, the briefest touch
as I sat in bed propped up
    drinking tea.

All right, it may not have been
a sudden rushing mighty wind
filling the house, but my skin
sensed it and took in the cool
fluky flow of air that I'm still
feeling the afterglow of
    days later.

House

Of course there are times it's a hearse –
polished, upholstered and proceeding
steadily towards its designated
parking space. Mostly though

it's my horse that pricks up its ears
as I drive in, trots across
for its carrot and can carry me off
where I please at the end of the day.

Or waking in the night, it's a freighter
I'm the master of, holding its course
through sheeting rain, a force eight;
or a purse and I'm in the money.

But just now and then a blink
and for better or worse what I've left
is a slight hollow in the grass
where a hare lies so still it's not there.

Birthday Cards

They vanish, as they must, soon enough
as if they've always been gathering dust
along the mantelpiece under the clock

till one day tidying for guests
you see them again, bring them back
into focus, all your cards on display –

this year, car workers in Detroit
by Diego Riviera, a Giacometti,
an Edwardian gent on a bike,

a bowl of quail's eggs in charcoal
and flowers and beaches and boats.
You clear them away, usher in

a future not featuring you.

According to Google

the cat's a hundred and three.
She's a relic of the boys' boyhood

bequeathed to us, like the pirate ship
in the attic, but not out of sight,

so she bulks much larger
in my mind than I like to admit,

as if I had nothing more urgent to do
than feed her, deal with her hit-or-miss

litter tray and my irritability
at how often, as soon as I settle,

right on cue she appears mewing
and rears up, snags her claws

on my thigh and – stretched out
now she can't leap – waits to be lifted.

I'm weighed down by her warmth in my lap,
her longevity. Every day

I imagine her gone, my unbothered
life, though I baulk at the thought

of her dying, the corpse, and in the end
acquiesce, stroking her boniness,

aware how soon I'll be seventy myself –
according to Google with ten years left.

The Hummers

We're a dreamy lot, we move smoothly
from bed to bathroom to kitchen –
filling and clicking the kettle,
bending for bowls, easing drawers
for cutlery. We don't even know
we do it, minds idling, we reach
for the knob of the cupboard
we open for the cereal packet
we tilt – wheat flakes, raisins and nuts
sliding randomly out. Fragments
of a tune we can no longer name,
a soundtrack our children grew up to
mock us for, and yet maybe
how we'll be fondly remembered.
Not for our passion for earthworms
or cricket or quadratic equations,
more for this breakfast humming,
intermittent, next to nothing.

Visiting

All this struggling January morning
though my mind's been elsewhere – poor thing,
glooming in that shrunken room
where your visit's ending and I sense
(for all your loving kindness)
in your voice, your stance, a certain
liveliness there's no disguising,
your relief to be done with me, gone,
key slipped into the ignition –
meanwhile, outside through the fog
eventually the flurries in the hedge
get to me, turn out to be
birds feeding on the berries
clustered the length of the whippy
cotoneaster laterals set swinging
by their weight as their claws grip,
their flapping – fieldfares they are,
and redwings passing through, my garden
for the moment meeting their need.

The Tiger

Lit up in the porch
                        her toothy smile
welcoming us   into our own home
        cold sausage rolls
                        and a salad somehow wrong.
Each summer returned
            summoned from somewhere
                        to look after Gran
who didn't cook.
                    Kes.
                        What kind of a name was that?
'Nurse Morley' she'd been   'Morley' to Gran
        in charge of the twins
                    Mum and Nin   and Dick and Len
                        at Shellhaven.
Nobody's nurse
            and not just strict and fierce
but vicious
        with the back of the hairbrush.
                        And come to this
a battered case
                    on the divan   in the attic room
at number 1   Southborough Road
        Surbiton
            a holiday
                    relief
                        taking care of Gran
who from time to time
            turning out stuff
                        would pass on a dress
with some wear in it yet.
            And us slipping past her
                        home at last
to our Saturday comics   mine The Tiger
        three instalments
                        of Roy of the Rovers.

The Morrison Shelter

Nella Last matters
too much to let her pass
unremarked, cowering
with George in the parlour under
the bolted steel table
as another blast
shudders the house,
shatters glass, shakes down
thumping great lumps
of plaster, lungfuls of dust
which Nella breathes in,
resigned now, calm,
her one regret – not
to have opened that tin
of cling peaches for tea.

Volunteers

Last season's potatoes, the ones I missed –
not digging or sifting thoroughly enough –
that disrupted my spinach and rose between
the rows of beans, are ready for lifting.

Volunteers they're called, you told me once
sharing your pleasure in the term
I remember again as another year's
gone since you kicked the chair away

to put yourself out of the misery
I would have done more to help you bear.
I slide the fork in wide to avoid
spiking or gashing any – fat chance.

Left Standing

These days mostly they're in cars
the dead, going past so fast
I hardly register more
than the tilt of a head, strong
chin, haggard neck or a grin.

Family and friends – today Nin
laughing at the wheel of a nippy
Fiat, overtaking a bus,
not that alive she could ever
be bothered with learning to drive.

Curt of course keeps flashing by,
but acquaintances too I'd forgotten
had died. And even if they glance
my way as we cross, they look
straight through me, they couldn't care less.

Character

Let's not forget this one either,
the burly bloke with the camouflage
trousers and moustache, the wild grey hair,

who lives out at the back of Pat's,
too big for the bike he rides bow-legged
or sometimes pushes up the slight incline

into town, where he tramps around
routinely morose, talking to no-one
but himself, though occasionally

over the years he's shouted the odd
threat or insult in my face as we've crossed
outside the chemist or the Greek.

Most recently startled me snarling
Town full of mongols as I thought-
lessly for a moment met his eye

and looked away, passed briskly by.

The Finishing Touch

Whatever brought me here
forgotten now **Ratafia**'s
caught my eye. Not **1**.
An almond-flavoured
cordial or liqueur
and not quite **2**. either
A kind of cake or biscuit
made to be eaten with it,
but rather what she called
those tiddly macaroons
she'd dot on the top of trifles.
Her dinner party standby
set aside in the pantry
to savour itself in Spode –
the sponge and the raspberry jam,
at first unconvinced, would reach
a consensus with the sherry
and the custard underneath
the whisked cream just beginning
to soften the very bottoms
of the blessed ratafias.
The least of her ingredients
and nothing on their own,
she kept them in a tin
I'd open always hoping
I might find something better.
Clearing the house that summer
I would have tipped them out
without a second thought.
We asked them not to treat
the chest infection. That
was it. She never spoke again.
And even in dreams she's cold,
knowing what she knows.

Lap

The children first, half a dozen
revved up to arrive at the seaside,
surge around where we sit on the pebbles.

In their wake the grown-ups with the gear,
giving us space, set up camp
not too near and gather them in,

all but one, a small boy, maybe three,
who stands between us and the sea
that holds him so long and so still

when at last he turns round and finds
us behind him, we won't forget
that all at sea look on his face,

the relief when he clocks his mistake
and scampers off back to his own
mum, settles himself in her lap.

Distress

Not that I'd want
to cause him pain,
quite the reverse,

yet here I am
playing it back,
revelling in it –

his look of distress
on learning we're leaving,
how soon we'll be gone.

Approaching

head down, swaying a little,
she's cycling into the wind
up the rise, her anorak flapping,
across her back something
strapped – a violin case
not full size. She's standing
on her pedals now, keeping going,
as we drive towards her, flash past –
twelve or thirteen, flushed, dishevelled
and in the rear-view mirror already
gone, carried away with her music.

Moment of Hope

Even in the dream I'm loath
to go there, though I know I must

take the scrubby path up through the gorse
to the clearing by the fence out of sight

of the house (our house, though I've never
been inside) where the rabbit hutches

persist – brittle roofing felt split,
water bottles spider-dry,

and, on sparse straw in the corner
at the back, droppings hard as shot.

The rusted hinges resisting
my cautious tug at a door

allow me a moment of hope
that this time I'll find them well

and truly dead, not needing help.

Ladybird, Ladybird

Must be this morning's at last
warm spring sunshine that's coaxed
these crumbs of comfort out
onto my south-facing window,
in some crevice or cranny of which
I imagine they've hibernated

clustered so tightly together
they can only stir and emerge
in ones or twos, so each time
I persuade them onto my sheet
of paper and return from shaking
them off outside the back door

there are more crawling across
impenetrable glass. It's cold
out of the sun for April,
too cold perhaps for aphids
or thrips, though what do I know
but to take them out, blow them away?

The Verge

Is it June maybe helps you see –
sunshine, no coat, less between
all these greens and your skin?
And the purple pink mauve and blue
flowers in the verge ringing bells,

insisting after all these years –
Comfrey, we're comfrey. And the grasses
that wave as you pass on your bike –
tall fescue, couch, cocksfoot and rye
shoulder high now and each distinct.

Could be it's the exercise, extra
blood supplied to your eyes,
or your mind, overdosed on death,
keen to light on an antidote.
Whatever the reasons, for once

you're alive to lush clumps of nettles,
thistles bristling, elder and mallow,
to ragwort, plantains and dock,
caught up in their swelling crescendo
as you ride down the road to your gate.

And at home now forget yourself,
flicking through the pages to check
if red stems, somewhat zigzag, alternate
oval leaves which come to a point
could fit with Japanese knotweed.

Unheard Of

Turning back to language with some idea
of the inexhaustible plenty there
restoring you, you're drawn in
on page one by **Abacinate**,
unheard of word, *v* for verb:
To blind by placing hot irons
or metal plates before the eyes,
rare according to the OED.

Bayonet

The etymology's doubtful,
it may derive from Bayonne,
where they first made them
or used them or else
from baion, Old French
for the shaft of a crossbow.
But everyone knows what it is –
a short flat steel dagger,
a stabbing instrument fixed
to the muzzle of a musket or rifle.
And we all know how to use it,
how to shove it in and twist
firmly – we've seen the films –
simple as changing a lightbulb.

Callipygian

A thought I have often enough
– it goes without saying – but not
a word I'd ever use
to express it. *Literary*
says the dictionary

but too clever by half for me,
calling attention to itself
when I want language transparent,
not obstructing our simply wonderful
view of such shapely buttocks.

February

Even now a crinkle of pleasure
writing or typing it out,
knowing its shape – how long

it must be since I learnt
not to forget that perverse
inaudible first r.

Ah, the last of the months
to come clean, it never
tripped me up again, the spelling.

Literate, pleased with myself,
whatever else – silent, unvoiced –
goes on passing me by.

Ignorance

I'll carry this with me each day
how at twenty in a library I happened
on photos I kept going back to
pore over, accounts of the camps
I read with a terrible thirst
I did my best to ignore.

One Life

Though not unaware of what's going on
in the Arctic Circle or Afghanistan

eager all the same to let you know
what I did today before I forget

the cherry stones I aimed and spat
at the grates in the gutter as I biked into town

three out of three sent skittering in.

Pull

More often these days I leave myself
accelerating out of a bend
or driving fast down a long straight:

as a truck, a coach or a couple
of cars approaching closes the gap,
I tighten my grip on the nubbled wheel

and foot pressed down I angle across
the crown of the road to crash
into anyone's horrified face –

a wrecking ball, an artillery shell,
buckled metal, jagged bone.
A blink and I'm past,

innocuous, easing
my breathing, my knuckles, my foot
off the pedal just a little.

Spontaneous

No apparent spark, not a suspicion
of smoke, but all at once
you combust, you're a crackle of knuckle,
desiccated michaelmas daisies,
a flare of spider and snail,
don't care, straw house ablaze.

Late

He'd gone for a chicken tikka.
I was waiting to take him to the film
parked by his hand-written sign
'shut the gate' in capitals, faded
ink on white card under cracked
polythene, the drawing-pins rusty.
Too impatient at the time to notice
how surprising, how he never did Indian
– *too spicy* – when he was alive.

Nails in the Coffin

a myth apparently
neither toe-
nor finger-nails
go on growing
after death

the truth though less
mysterious
palpably
makes perfect
sense

blood
no longer pumped
sinks back
and so the skin
around them shrinks

Ladder

Forget climbing up
among apples or,
more conspicuous,
fixing a loose
slate on the roof.
This one goes down
who knows how deep,
a whole other world
that stinks of rot
and rust, and worse,
though most at first,
you'll get used to it.
Why would you think
you'd be exempt?
Lower yourself
into the shaft –
the rungs ought
to take your weight.

Deathtrap

Leaning forward as I bike into town
this morning it's George Curtis
I become for a moment –
that keen judicious frown,
the exact angle of his head.

Over forty years unbeknown
to me my muscle memory's
stored the way he'd stand
planning our future, this dead
eager father of my dead friend,

still fizzing in my stiffening body,
the gin and tonic he insists
I hold out for him to freshen –
so cheers, old body, relax,
after all not just a deathtrap.

The 39th Wedding Anniversary

Together in bed afterwards:
Remember the shed, she said,
what's his name's. And I did –
how he'd made a boat of it,
loaded up the surplus bits
and paddled it down the Rhine
some seven miles into Basel
where he reassembled it
and made it look just the same
staid old shed it was before.

Together

Even when I rub her back
in bed sometimes, when my hand
curves over a shoulder blade
or the tips of my fingers affirm
her warm breathing skin and follow
the course of her vertebrae down
the long valley of her spine;
even then, so close to her all
but inaudible sigh of wellbeing,
I miss her, I grieve for her, ache
for the small of her back I'm actually
making much of, stroking – better
pull yourself together, mgl.

Breakfast

Though I can't ask of course
what it all comes down to is this –
as you pass behind my chair
with your cereal bowl, how my turned
back aches for your touch.

In the Moment

Cycling home across what we call
the aerodrome, though that's long gone,
almost always I remember the hare,
how it loped on ahead of me there
a hundred yards straight down the road
till it stopped and turned and stared
and at my approach lolloped off
between rows of beans out of sight.
I can see it now, unlike
yesterday when a jag of pain
in my left knee transported me
smack into the moment – not always
all it's cracked up to be.

Treatment

Back in hospital again today,
no fun, but let's hear it for the porter
who stopped and asked was I lost.

And for the old boy I was sat next to
whose affability lightened
the wait in that windowless room.

He told me he'd worked from fourteen
on a fruit farm; how to save blackcurrants
from frost, they'd burn fuel oil in drums

all across the field, smoke it off.
With greengages though, how each tree
comes up with a bumper crop

every seventh year, never fails;
how unpropped branches breaking
will make it make new growth.

At Your Feet

Your first sighting this May morning
of the white hoop of a French bean bent
on straightening up means there'll be more
surfacing as you peer down the row,
means summer suppers on the step,
salade niçoise, an elation of swifts
over your head, but for now at your feet
here's another one coming through braced
to shake off the weight of soil and hoist
creased moist leaves, a bean that's already
split its own skin and grown out of itself.

Living with Lemons

In the beginning the word
was yours by heart even before
the honey and lemon your mother
would bring to your bedside and sit
you up to sip at, to soothe
a cough or loosen the thick
phlegm on your chest, filling
your mouth with mucus, another
good word you've done nothing to deserve.

❋

You know we've exhausted the planet,
practically milked it dry,
nevertheless go on thinking
the metaphor still holds good –
that the blossom end of the lemon's
a nipple, as Neruda had it.

❋

Coming in from the overcast night
the lemon's a memo the moon's
still with us, just out of sight.

❋

Not that old story of the boy
baffled by his first banana
after the war. Instead
imagine the tang
of citrus rising again
from the hold, your appetite whetted

for peace and its prospects, not least
the crate the dockers will duly
smash for divvying up.

✳

If your boy's a man now, decades
on from childhood, you'll know
you're blessed when across the room
– *catch* – he tosses you a lemon.

✳

The poem you're writing excites
another, you make a note.
Lemon trees do it too: fruit
and flower at the same time.

✳

It was citron pressé your mother
knew and introduced you to
in the shade of a pavement café
in a square that scorching day
driving south, the day you learnt
what thirst and quench really meant.

✳

When the time comes to express
the juice it's right and fitting
that the lemon-squeezer placed
on the worktop is solid glass
and gleams like a chandelier.

✳

Mind what happens to the spare
half of the lemon – how soon
left to itself the cut seals.

※

Lemon juice gives that edge
to sweetness who doesn't want
in a fresh fruit salad, or love?
Added to the syrup it keeps
the crisp slices of apple
– bananas too, if you must –
from ending up mostly browned off.

※

If it's something you're lacking, zest,
it might help to remind yourself
that the word derives from Old French
for lemon peel, which must mean
you've actually got some – surely
you always keep a lemon in?

※

Unlike Sydney Smith, who moved
in 1808 to his living
at Foston-le-Clay, a place
'so far out of the way'
he wrote to friends in London
'I am twelve miles from a lemon'.

Aubergine

*Aubergine, the French name of the egg-plant, is now known to
some extent in Britain by its purple fruit about the size of a small
fist. It is listed in the Concise Oxford Dictionary of 1950. How it is
pronounced in English is another matter.*
The Changing English Language – *Brian Foster 1968*

Here in 2012, thoroughly at home,
grown in our own polytunnels,
more gravid pear than small fist,
and causing no stir alongside
cauliflowers and carrots,
you're the bright idea
I was after for supper tonight –
stuffed with chick peas and served
with French beans now they're coming on stream,
we'll pronounce you perfectly delicious.

Mood

Sometimes it works,
a few words
get through, can
change your mood.

Like today
chalked up
on the A-board
outside Bertie's:
'Hair cut
while you wait'

Chopping Board

It's maple, according to the friend
who made it for me who knows how
many years ago, though I've never
noticed till now its neat
bevelled edges or how little heed
I've paid to the difference it makes
to my day, the lift it gives me

just to pick it up. Thick as my thumb's
top joint and the weight of a bottle
of wine, I'm always laying it down
on the worktop – a buoyancy aid
or a stage set for precise
cucumber slicing, for seeing
how finely I can dice an onion.

Must be a hardwood – streaked
both sides by all those knives
but so close-grained, it's smooth.
Cut out for dance-floors, it used
to be used too, says the book,
for cotton reels I'd forgotten
my hand once knew would be wood.

Instead it lives in the kitchen
beside our flashy new kettle,
ready for whatever comes next –
an oblong slab, good and solid
for bearing down on, mindful
of yet more windfall Bramleys
to core and peel and purée.

On the Desk

the stapler too waits its turn
to come in, to embody once more

the feeling of the heel of the hand
pressed down, teeth clenched, and released

so these loose cornered sheets combine.
Low tech, instant cause and effect,

unless it's run out, when the dent
in the paper's your prompt to click

the catch at the back and the spring-
loaded magazine emerges.

In the cluttered drawer you uncover
the box of the right staples, packed

in strips inside one another.
How neatly they fit. Slide it shut.

And it's fixed, primed again to come
down firmly against non-attachment.

Curtains

Faded red velvet, double-sided,
they fall to the floor in the bay,
they've hung in all our front rooms,
stretch back even further, passed on
by Auntie Ethel from your grandma,
the Methodist Recorder crossword one.

Despite what they do to the light
twice a day, and the stereo screak
of metal, tiny wheels on the rail
(came with the house, an antique),
as we slide them open or shut,
we're hardly conscious of them, drawn

more to the traffic, the rain-slicked
tarmac, the flickering ash tree,
or turned already towards supper.
So though I know they don't let
any light through (so thick you'd think,
from the street at night, nobody's in)

yet now I notice how thin,
actual holes, a small split in each one
at the edge, just where reaching up
(arms wide as if blessing the outside)
I take hold and tug them across,
tweak again so they overlap,

don't leave that gap at the top.
Worn, but so what? They're part
of the one flesh we've become.
Let them hang on here and declare
another day open, then put it
behind them, bring the evening on.

Perm

It wasn't of course. You grew
it out quite soon. Too much
of a fiddle with work
and two small boys. Maybe
you weren't so keen on the look
anyway, though I loved
all those curls, such flamboyance.
No need for the golden
thirty-something-year-old
photo of the three of you
on the verge of the faded
cornfield picnicking.
I haven't forgotten it yet.
How much more permanent
than that can you get?

Lucky

Before bed a breath of air
outside the back door.
A new moon
sails between clouds
and you murmur
Must cut my nails.

Swifts

1.

Each May warming to it, you keep
an eye out for them, you scan
reedbeds and treetops and banks
of slow cloud for the first to arrive,
you write down the date and count
        yourself lucky

that they nest in your eaves and for weeks
whenever you tilt your head back
even tiny, they fill the skies
and at dusk so much more, a headlong
throng of them screaming round the house,
        such a din

it's the silence eventually which
makes itself heard and gets through
to you and you know it's true –
they've already gone and summer's
as good as over, though August's
        hardly begun.

2.

A man, a woman and the swifts are one.
What do they come to if the swifts are gone?

Service

Such a racket when it's on,
so much clatter and din,
it can drown out even the drilling
phone beyond the glass door
in the alcove under the stairs.
(We must bring it through on its long
lead – handy, with all that clanking,
for walking anyone who calls
back into the audible hall.)

It's old okay, installed here
like us more than thirty years,
but still clicks and cranks itself up
at set times. Before the alarm
its distant rattles and thumps
rise through the house and gently
knock at our sleep, remind us
day's coming with its hot water
and weather it will help us weather.

On his knees and spanner in hand,
Peter Goddard, bless him, says not
to scrap it, why would you
when it works and you're lucky
if a new combi lasts seven years?
Obsolete, our Ideal E type,
with the 'I' all but gone on its nameplate
and the brilliant white casing
matt at best or baked brown.

Not long and he's done, he vacuums
twelve months of slut's wool,
slots the front back on and leaves
the pilot light he's reignited
burning for us out of sight.
Later, relaxed in the warm
silence, the boiler switched off,
we're spooked by a loud *croo-croo*
just behind us, down the silver flue.

Footpath

Walking it's
no great shakes
minimum
exercise
on a day
spent inside
nothing much
noteworthy
almshouses
in a row
with their line
of Scots pines
mind your feet
up ahead
pylons lope
fizz in mist
traffic noise
east and west
a slight slope
down towards
an always
boggy bit
to skirt round
where run-off
stands on clay
lots of sky
at least some
five hundred
yards across
the field
through the crops
winter wheat
potatoes
rape or beet

ripening
harvested
and at once
the land ploughed
and re-sown
the footpath's
gone all one
regular
drilled expanse
good to see
how soon feet
track across
flatten it
put it back
on the map
OS sheet
156
a ruled red
dotted line
but in fact
what you love
more's the view
from the gap
in the hedge
how it bends
right and left
deviates
from the straight
finds itself
moving you
like a tune
an old song
no-one knows
who wrote or
for certain
quite how it
ought to go

Scots Pine

Though it grows in the garden
                        it's hardly ours –
despite the bat box
             hammered home
                   facing south
as high up the trunk
           as the ladder would reach;
or the rope
           I climbed out higher still
        on the thickest branch,
                 agile   ages ago
to secure
           for the boys
               to tarzan on;
and despite the cones
           Kay likes to collect
                   (less tax
than involuntary contribution)
             and burn on our open fire
                  for the smell.

Taller than
           this 1920s house
and here from the first
           I'd guess
               from the girth
            my arms can't encompass,
it stands
         to one side,
              overlooks us,
                  focused
on its straight trunk,
            its lop-sided tops,

on extending itself
            further over
                        the hedge   and on
apparently well
            into the next
                        century.
Raggedy blue-green
            needle canopy.
                        Red bark
        catching the first
                        and last of the light.
But my favourite
            most for its
                        asymmetry,
for the jagged
                    branch ends
                            broken off,
the impossible
            limbs it will keep
                        going out on.

Seeds

Two of them, caught on the weave
of his shorts, like dandelions' only small,
ragwort perhaps or thistles
brushed past as he climbed the cliff path,

and for a moment before he starts
the car, he's no-one, an unwitting medium-
sized furred animal spreading
some sort of wildflower or weed.

Going the Extra Mile

Nothing wrong with a routine ride
for bread or milk. Good too
to cycle with Kay, though that's always
a bit of a business, her tyres to pump
while she changes and then the palaver

over where – *No, you choose.*
Simpler just pushing off
by myself, no definite plan,
letting the wind, say, decide
which way to turn at the gate.

An hour will do, a few miles
on back roads, some of the best
embedded with moss, single track,
and on paths through gorse, through woods,
across fields of pigs to the sea.

But even now and then coming close
to deer or a barn owl is less
of a blessing than those moments
at any cross-roads or fork
or bridleway branching off

when without thinking twice
I change course, pedalling the new
route home in my head, alive
to my legs on their mettle, going
the extra mile, pleasing myself.

Resolutions

with the new year every year
a surge in submissions   dear sir/
madam   please consider   hope
you enjoy   bending to the heap
of plump brown and white C5
and C4 crossed fingers fanned out
on the mat   nine ten some days
more   such resolve arrived
at independently deserves
some thought   but first of all
I flick through for any
smaller thinner letters
caught up in the pile   the odd
one or two who've decided
to subscribe now or renew

A Bundle of Bamboos

Lashed top and bottom with bleached
garden string in the autumn and parked
by the mast of Kay's dinghy between
the rafters in the garage, it catches
my eye as I back out the car
fast on this pinched March morning

and at once my fingers itch
to unpack the kit and erect it
on the veg patch, imagine they might
remember the dream-neat knots
at the intersections, how long
each piece of string needs to be.

What I want are runner beans
to swarm up and cover the frame,
lavish leaves, flowers, nodding pods –
Scarlet Emperor please, or Polestar.
In the last of the sun I'm setting
the fruit, thumbing a fine spray

from the hose at the tent, see how
I reach out now and jiggle a cane
so any still invisible bean
will swing like the tongue of a bell.
All this and more, *if I'm spared*,
as my mother used to say, looking forward.

Waiting for the Wave

Perhaps that's the secret, the archive
recording of Edwin Morgan,
what he said last week on Last Word:
(which I caught washing up and went on
cleaning the top of the cooker to)
that what interested him was the future.

Which reminds me, it's time to check
on my earlies, Arran Pilots, laid out
on the boogie board I fetched in
from the garage to Tim's old room
(light and cool with the radiator off) –
should be a good place to sprout them.

Weighing the Present

I didn't believe it for a minute
but turning the corner at the lights
saw him waiting on the opposite pavement
outside A1 Discounts to cross.

Though I didn't believe it for a moment
I knew it was him by the set
of his shoulders and head, that physique
and the all but forgotten lift

of my heart at the sight of him.
For an instant he was alive
or I had died, though I knew
neither could be true and pressed on

to the post office past my friend
with the present that needed weighing,
more or less knowing nothing
was impossible, even heaven.